LONDON TRANSPORT

Buses and Coaches

1951

LONDON TRANSPORT
BUSES & COACHES

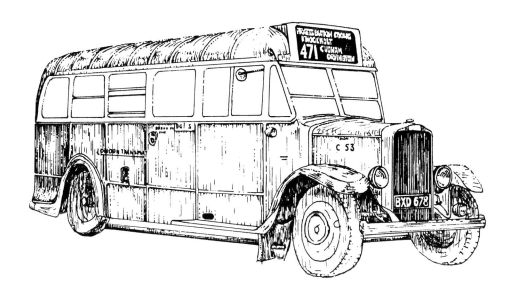

1951

John A.S. Hambley

Published 1992 by
The Self Publishing Association Ltd
Units 7/10, Hanley Workshops,
Hanley Road, Hanley Swan,
Worcs.

A MEMBER OF

in conjunction with
JOHN A.S. HAMBLEY
7 Linden Road,
Dunstable,
Beds. LU5 4NZ

British Library Cataloguing in Publication Data

A catalogue record for this book is available
from the British Library

ISBN 1 85421 164 1

Front cover photograph:

This nice view of C34 reminds one of the position of the used ticket box on these small saloons. The fleet number is underneath the ticket box together with the last overhaul date and what appears to be a later date when paintwork was touched up. In the background is the Southern Region's Dorking North Station and a Bedford OB with austerity bus bodywork completes the picture. The destination COLDHARBOUR FOR "LEITH HILL" is rather quaint and one wonders why the blind compiler felt it necessary to use inverted commas. (Lens of Sutton)

Back cover photograph:

A finishing touch to this book for 1951, is this picture of LTC24, the ultimate coach of this pre-war luxury class.

Designed and Produced by Images Design and Print Ltd
Printed and Bound in Great Britain by Ebenezer Baylis

Acknowledgements

Once again it gives me great pleasure to thank everyone who, in one way or another, have helped me to publish this latest edition, be it with their personal contribution of photographs or their time and energy in helping caption the prints. These have included:

James Aston, J.F. Bearman, Ronald G. Bristow, C. Carter, Alan B. Cross, J.C. Gillham, W.J. Haynes, the late J.F. Higham via Reg Westgate, D.W.K. Jones, Kevin Lane, S.E. Letts, Sheila Taylor of the London Transport Museum, Roy Marshall, Geoff Morant, John Pilgrim, J.H. Price, G.A. Rixon, David A. Ruddom, Lyndon Rowe, D. Trevor Rowe, R.H.G. Simpson, John Smith of Lens of Sutton, John G.S. Smith and S. Sponheimer. My wife, Iris, for all her typing abilities, patience and tolerance and last but not least the P.S.V. Circle whose excellent range of publications have been used as the basis for the captions.

Any photograph not identified with an owners name or a collection from which it has been used are from the author's own comprehensive collection, which has been built up over many years of interest in the buses and coaches of London Transport. I would be very pleased to hear from any photographer, not credited, who identifies his work so that due acknowledgement can be made in future books within the series.

Publisher's Note

Many photographers, have either let me know that they have prints suitable for later years in this series of books or have sent me copies of prints for viewing to ascertain their quality for possible use as material for books now being assembled.

As I have mentioned in previous books, if you do have prints, or even just a solitary print, appropriate to the subject and which would be interesting to other enthusiasts, then please do not keep them to yourself. Even if you only have the negative, arrangements can be made for Kevin Lane, the black and white printing specialist, to provide a suitable print.

It is surprising how the memory fades and it has given me, together with Dave Ruddom and John G.S. Smith, many wonderful hours of nostalgia looking though suitable photographs to include and caption in any one book. I sincerely hope you, the enthusiast, find the same enchantment looking through the pages that follow.

Introduction

This is the third book in the series looking at buses and coaches which were once operated by London Transport. Before going any further I would like to apologise for a small number of typographical errors which appeared in the first print run of the 1950 volume. Steps have been taken to prevent a recurrence in future books of the series.

The year now covered, as with previous years, had a number of highlights. The first of these was the Festival of Britain. Several new services were introduced for the benefit of the tourist who would want to visit the various sites within the Capital which were being used as part of the Festival. Included in this book are a number of photographs showing some of these special services that the visitor could use. Many STLs, which might otherwise have been disposed of, were overhauled and tucked away unlicensed at various places in the months leading up to the festivities, at which time they were called upon to perform on either these special services or as extras on existing routes to help move the vast number of visitors around. It is perhaps worth reminding younger readers that car ownership was not yet a common thing. The result was another interesting period of photography for bus enthusiasts.

The tram replacement by diesel bus programme progressed at a steady pace during the year. The four stages which occurred during 1951 removed trams from the streets of south west London; the main road through Streatham and Croydon; Bermondsey and Rotherhithe as well as the notorious four tracked Dog Kennel Hill and leafy Dulwich. As a result many new bus routes were inaugurated, some on roads unfamiliar to this form of transport and, sadly, many trams were withdrawn from service with the older examples in the fleet being scrapped.

The Eastern National local operations in and around the Grays area were taken over by London Transport Executive on 30 September, 1951 and a varied selection of Eastern National vehicles could be seen in the area bearing the London Transport fleetname although still in Eastern National green. In addition a number of spare STLs were drafted in to help out through the transitional period before the routes were fully integrated into the London Transport Country Area network. Again, a number of photographs appear in the book of these historic three months.

Deliveries of new vehicles continued as in the previous years, there being no let up yet in the considerable numbers being added to the fleet. Replacement continued of the earlier bus and coach classes introduced both pre-war and during the war years and the continuing programme of tram replacement kept pace. This, together with the whole of the bus industry being in an expansion period, meant much change on the streets of London.

Two new classes of coaches appeared on the road during the year, the RF and the RFW, both of which utilized the AEC underfloor engined Regal Mark IV chassis. Bodywork was provided by Metro Cammell for the 700 strong fleet of RFs which were to be delivered over a three year period. A very unmistakable Eastern Coachworks 39 seat body was built for the 15 strong RFW class. Both classes had the entrance incorporated ahead of the first set of road wheels and directly opposite the driver. In the case of the RF class seating was provided for a varied number of passengers in line with the intended use for which they were built.

For the year then, a further 222 STL type were withdrawn from service together with two more of the ST class, these two being of the lowbridge variety. A solitary single deck LT and one member of the T class were withdrawn. The little Leyland Cub C class of vehicles lost another nine, all of which were of the Inter-station type and represented the last remaining petrol driven vehicles in the fleet, whilst the first eighteen of the six-wheeled LTC coach class were also lost to the streets of London. Witnessed during the year was the first withdrawals of the Bristol B class, five in total going together with the entire eleven of the wartime delivered STDs. The austerity class to be hit hardest by withdrawals was the Guy Arab G class where no less than 163 of this utility type of bus were withdrawn. One of the pre-war RTs was also withdrawn after an accident on the ice of Wimbledon Hill in January of that year. The total number of buses and coaches withdrawn for the year then amounted to only 533, a somewhat lesser number than in previous years, but some of the reasons for this have been mentioned above.

New vehicles delivered for the year amounted to 1233, being made up of 890 RT class buses (577 from Weymann, 312 from Park Royal with the last solitary example from Saunders); 217 RTL class buses (34 from Metro-Cammell and 183 from Park Royal); all 15 of the new class of high specification RFW coaches from ECW and finally the first 111 of the RF class coaches. This latter delivery meant that many vehicles hitherto used for this type of work could be put to new uses.

Festival routes G and H were provided as what today would be called "Park and Ride" services to the South Bank and Festival Gardens respectively. Neither did any trade worth mentioning and both were very quickly withdrawn. Here a bored looking driver surveys the photographer and the inspectors wonder whether another journey is really necessary for STL1699. (A.B. Cross)

Sidcup's T761 is seen here at Well Hall, Eltham destined for Chislehurst War Memorial, a point short of the full 228 route to the Gordon Arms. This style of blind display was standard for LT single deckers in the Central Area from pre-war days and the comprehensive route details, unlike double deck displays, survived throughout the war and were only removed, presumably in the interests of clarity, in the 1950s when the new RF vehicles arrived. (R.G. Bristow)

Victoria Station forecourt in the days before the addition of the utilitarian structure which now sits over the bays. All the buildings in the background still stand to this day, though you will not see an Achille Serre Quality Cleaners and Dyers delivery van anymore. SRT52, whose chassis once belonged to STL2610, waits with RT2296 in this 31st May scene. (J.H. Aston)

Seen on a nice sunny day at Uxbridge Station, STL1558 waits to leave on Excursion 6, one of the Circular Tours of London arranged during the year from outer parts of the capital to see the Festival of Britain sights. Despite having an allocation of RTs the excursionists were given a 15 year old vehicle by Uxbridge garage in which to tour. (A.B. Cross)

One of the lowbridge variety STL class standing at Staines West Station awaits to commence its next duty on the 436 route to Guildford. STL1047 was eventually sold to W. North (dealer) of Leeds for scrapping.

C74 picks up the shoppers in Hoddesdon before making its way to Harlow on the 393 route then operated by Epping garage. The stop behind the bus appears to be disused on account of its proximity to a new pedestrian crossing. (A.B. Cross)

STD159 is pictured here passing Parliament Square on its fairly long journey from Kings Cross to Raynes Park on Route 77A. (Roy Marshall)

STL2134 on route 49 and the RT on route 133, both of which await their drivers, appear to be causing the RT on route 19 further along the road a problem, the driver of which is probably muttering to himself "I wish somebody would move so I can get my cuppa". The scene is the stand at The Greyhound, Streatham Common and the presence of a 19 indicates a Sunday or Bank Holiday. Note that the lack of blind masking on the STL, which has probably been used on Festival services, has caused another problem, particularly as the bus is working short and not serving Crystal Palace. (J.G.S. Smith collection)

Chalk Farm's SRT147 is seen here in Pimlico whilst operating on Route 24. This bus made use of the chassis of STL2041, originally a 4/9STL variety which when new carried a metal framed Park Royal body from the same manufacturer as the one now carried. (Roy Marshall)

The conductor has not yet changed the number blind to 457C – perhaps he never will – for this short trip to Pinewood Studios on the irregular service which served that famous film location. Craven bodied RT1426, itself looking a picture, stands at Uxbridge at a point that is now virtually in the new garage entrance. (Geoff Morant)

Followed by a lowbridge STL on route 410, Q50, working back to its base at Dunton Green, awaits departure at Bromley North. The lack of a running number suggests this may be an additional working, in this picture taken on the 25th May. (J.H. Aston)

The Salvation Army Hall on the east side of Hertford Bus Station forms part of the country town background for 10T10, T477 still carrying Green Line fleetnames. Now relegated to ordinary country bus services for its last couple of years service with London Transport it departs to the eastern borders of Hertfordshire at Sawbridgeworth. (Geoff Morant)

Weymann bodied STL1493 now with the body originally carried by the first of this batch of 50 vehicles, STL1475. It is seen here at the Wrotham terminus of route 478 which ran from Swanley Station and which started as a wartime Green Line replacement route but survived the re-introduction of Green Line services. (W.J. Haynes)

STL471 is working Festival Route F on a typical Festival of Britain wet day. The dolly type bus stop with information for potential bus users was a common feature throughout the period of the festivities. The stop is in fact for the short lived Route H which served the Patmore Street car park rather than Route F to the far more popular Clapham Common coach parks.

The George and Dragon at Linford provides the background to a Guy Arab I carrying Brush lowbridge bodywork for 55 seated passengers. This bus, 3875, was the lowest numbered of the Guy Arabs which were transferred to London Transport. (J.C. Gillham)

The ultimate numbered vehicle of this very small class was RFW15. These coaches were used chiefly on long distance private hire work. Interestingly this type of body was very uncommon with only another small batch of similar type being built for Tillings Transport.

Fairly new RT4204, showing evidence of the traditional dirty roads by the cement works near Swanscombe, puts in a turn as a Green Line relief on a wet and deserted late summer running on route 701 to Gravesend. The lovely original canopied roof line to Victoria Station is alas no longer with us and nowadays the bus would be facing the wrong way on a one way street. (Roy Marshall)

AEC Regent chassised STL1447 is followed by another vehicle from the same manufacturer in the shape of an AEC Mammoth Major. The body carried by this bus has obviously been re-domed at some stage since it carries a roof box as well as provision for three displays between decks. Pictured here in Southall with a bill poster at work on the Gaumont Cinema behind, the bus was to survive at Alperton garage in passenger service for a further year until November 1952. It then became a first aid lecture room, at Hertford garage for the LTE ambulance section of the St. John's Ambulance Brigade until March 1958. (A.B. Cross)

Another lively scene at North Street, Romford, with STL442 leading on route 66 from Leytonstone followed by City Coach Company's LT15, a Leyland TS7T (registration CXW440) rebodied by Heaver in 1947, bound for Southend from Wood Green. (A.B. Cross)

The Railway Lost Property Sales Department and the decorative lamp post confirm this picture as having been taken at Charing Cross. The entrance to Strand Underground Station on the Northern Line can be seen at the left edge of the picture. The ABC sign above STL450 marks the premises of a branch of the Aerated Bread Company, a well patronized tea shop and bakers of the era, which was a slightly down market competitor to "Joe Lyons". (A.B. Cross)

Operating from Watford High Street garage is STL2695 seen here on a short working of the 351 route which, at its full length, ran from Harpenden to Uxbridge. This batch of 20 Weymann bodied vehicles only worked in London for nine years so it was not surprising that when they were withdrawn they all found new homes with various municipal corporations. (A.B. Cross)

STL1543 is operating on one of the special Festival of Britain services. Route C ran between the South Bank Exhibition at Waterloo and the Festival Gardens at Battersea Park where this photograph was taken. This STL is coded 3/9STL11 and was withdrawn from service later in the year. The vehicle is operating from Peckham garage which only opened in May and was not usually associated with this type. (A.B. Cross)

A superb view of 9T9 Country Area bus T450 standing at Staines on the 26th August in company with two Hounslow RTs (879 and 832). The T bus carries a Weymann built coach body with seating for 30 passengers. The chassis is an AEC Regal with 7.7 litre oil engine, fluid transmission and hydraulic breaking. Of note for a heavyweight vehicle built in 1936 is the use of a front bumper, a feature carried only on these 9T9 vehicles together with the LTC class and varied numbers of the C class. (J.H. Aston)

The date is 16th September and C53 looks splendid in this early autumn view. This scene at Orpington Station is remarkably unchanged today, although in 1951 there was at least an inadequate shelter which the stand lacks completely today. (J.H. Aston)

Upton Park garaged RTW401, an all Leyland product, with canopy blind set for route 15, waits for work of some description on 11th September. This was a month after the 15 route was converted to this wider class of vehicle. (J.H. Aston)

STD164 turns to pass over the River Thames on Lambeth Bridge on its way to Raynes Park. At the top of the driver's door can be seen just one ventilator opening. Elsewhere in the book, you will find a picture of a similar vehicle with two openings. (Roy Marshall)

RT1867 turns the corner at Thornton Heath Pond about to pass the Harlequin Ice Cream "lounge", which seems to be a fancy name for a "caff". The crowded destination blind with the use of "ONLY" is incorrect since at this time route 190 went no further than the Swan and Sugar Loaf in any case. (Roy Marshall)

Weymann bodied G388 stands next to Baring House on the old Stainsby Street stand at Limehouse on 12th May. Those were the days when if you used a telephone box, it was red and you were protected from the elements while you made your call. (J.H. Aston)

Now a showman's bus this was once front entrance STL1037. As can be seen very clearly in this photograph, an offside hinged door has been added halfway along the length of the vehicle as has a door to the driver's cab. One window is now boarded up and others appear to be painted over but otherwise it is as withdrawn from service right down to the partially masked route indicator box. (R.H.G. Simpson)

Penhall Road, Charlton scrapyard, or "tramatorium" as some called it, on 8th July and front entrance STLs 963 and 1490 await their eventual scrapping by Messrs. Cohen. STL963 had just completed two months learner duties working from Hounslow garage whilst STL1490 was last used on passenger service at Hertford. (Lyndon Rowe)

Elderly Bristol J05G with ECW rear entrance bus bodywork for 31 passengers waits here at Grays for its journey out to Bulphan. As with all these loans, London Transport fleet names were applied together with the holders for garage and running number stencils. The bus carries red painted stencils GY 12 which was the normal practice to distinguish Argent Street operations from the Executive's own premises at Hogg Lane. (C. Carter)

LT1123 on route 227 from Elmers End garage is seen here negotiating the famous landmark of the Chislehurst Arch on 17th March. Unfortunately, or fortunately depending on your view, the structure which was built in 1860 as a water tower with two dwellings, one each side of the arch, was pulled down in 1963 and so this fine view of an elegant traffic hazard is but a memory now. (J.H. Price)

In 1951 TFs were regular Green Line performers from garages such as Epping, Dorking, Grays, Luton and St. Albans and, perhaps because of this, it would appear few photographs were taken of them. On Christmas Eve however, TF18 of Dorking was working the 425 short journeys to Westcott on a rather wet day. (A.B. Cross)

Seen passing the old Playhouse cinema built in the 1920s and demolished in the late 50s, B24 arrives at Greenford on route 97. The fuel feed system using the square tank underneath the front lower bulkhead window is clearly shown in this picture as too is the Margaret Thatcher look-alike above it! (A.B. Cross)

The date is 20th December, with very few shopping days left for Christmas, but where are the seasonal decorations and the gift laden shoppers in this view taken at Hemel Hempstead. Tree lopper 648J which was once ST1001 had quite a chequered career. Being originally built for Thomas Tilling Ltd. in 1931 the bus passed to the L.P.T.B. in October 1933. Part of 1942 and 1943 was spent on loan to Bournemouth Corporation and after its return to London it was converted to its new role as a tree lopper, being finally withdrawn and disposed of to Moore and Porter, dealers of Mitcham in 1953. (A.B. Cross)

Craven bodied RT1466 picks up passengers at Romford on market day whilst operating to Chadwell Heath in this July view. Judging by the many pedestrians wearing their top coats the hole in the ozone layer and the warm up of the World had not yet begun. (A.B. Cross)

RF124, although not delivered till January of 1952, typifies the new order of coaches now spreading rapidly through the Green Line network. Seen here on Eccleston Bridge as the author likes to remember this photographer's paradise for coaches. (Roy Marshall)

RT use on route 159 meant the withdrawal of the STL class from this service. Seen here in the leafy surrounds of the southern section of the route, RT455, a Weymann bodied RT3 type, works from Croydon garage having been delivered in 1947 and still to have its first overhaul.

(Lens of Sutton)

9STL5, STL704 operates from Elmers End garage on a Festival short working on Route 12 which is a replica of the famous Thomas Tilling service of early motorbus days. As with so many STL type vehicles this one had been overhauled a few months earlier and then was kept in store – in this case at Stansted Airport – until the opening of the Festival Season. The bus stands at the Oxford Circus terminus. (J.G.S. Smith collection)

A relatively new RT1956 operating on route 70, has come to grief at Waterloo lay-by and the Camberwell garage engineers have grabbed a split duty 137 to carry out a rescue. The fact that they have not reset the blinds might have caused some passengers confusion. RT4156 beyond also works route 70. (J.H. Aston)

Always a 9STL5, STL631 has been transferred from Festival of Britain services to Barking garage as evidenced by the awkward use of the restricted aperture blind. The bottom of the glass needs masking since the Festival blinds used the whole aperture. At this time surplus STLs were being transferred into Barking to replace the somewhat newer but more spartan Guy Arabs. (A.B. Cross)

Pre-war RTs were once a common sight on the 37 route from Hounslow to Peckham. Appropriately numbered RT37 has just pulled away from the Arding and Hobbs department store at Clapham Junction, brazenly advertising one of their competitors.

STL411 is a 2/16STL18 seen here at Hertford Bus Station on service 331 to Buntingford. This bus was scrapped just two years after this photograph was taken. (Geoff Morant)

STL1557 working a Festival Extra on route 68 negotiates the roundabout at the south end of Waterloo Bridge. In the background stands St. John's Church, Waterloo Road which, in 1951, was designated "The Festival Church" since the main exhibition site was within its parish. (A.B. Cross)

Seen entering Piccadilly Circus from Lower Regent Street and followed by a French import in the shape of a Citroen Traction Avant car, STL1332, like so many buses in 1951, carries an EXTRA slipboard on the nearside front window under the canopy but uses "proper" blinds rather than the more usual double ended variety for these Festival of Britain workings. (A.B. Cross)

At Peckham garage forecourt RT1239 from Nunhead garage awaits its next journey on route 37 with another RT behind on the same route, whilst to the right a Peckham RT awaits its duty on route 36.

In November, STL570 stands outside the Grays Conservative Club in Clarence Road. This was one of the red STLs drafted into the area and which was soon repainted into Country Area green. The red painted garage plates are discernible in this shot. Route 37A ran via Chadwell St. Mary to the then busy Tilbury Ferry for Gravesend and was to be tagged on to the long standing 370 Romford – Grays service when the routes were co-ordinated. (J.F. Higham)

Northern Counties bodied G240 is seen working route 101's summer Sunday extension beyond Wanstead to Lambourne End. This was a popular destination for East End day trippers but nowadays it is served only by the private cars of those trippers' descendants. (J.G.S. Smith collection)

Only six of the batch of eighty-five 15STL16 type buses escaped being converted to SRTs during 1949 and here lucky STL2543 puts in a relief journey on Green Line route 703 to Wrotham. The bus is seen outside its home garage at Swanley Junction. The body still had a life of several years ahead. After the bus was sold to the dealer, W. North of Leeds, it was acquired by B. Margo of Bexleyheath who fitted the body to the chassis of former STL2147 and it continued to operate in its new guise until February 1958.

With the buildings of Staines Central Station as a backdrop, STL564 operates from Staines garage on route 460 to Slough Station. (A.B. Cross)

Highbridge and lowbridge variety buses operate route 410 on the 2nd June at Reigate. This arrangement was necessary as RLH20 is working the full route to Bromley North Station on which it will encounter the low bridge at Oxted, while RT3143 behind is on a short working, probably to Godstone, although as yet the driver has not reset the destination blind. (J.H. Aston)

A scene not much changed to this day, although a new bridge now spans the cutting and many trees have disappeared. Park Royal bodied D247 operating along the main road between Sutton and Rose Hill, spent its entire London service in this area of South West London operating from Sutton garage. (Lens of Sutton)

Both these pictures were taken on the 11th June at Golders Green and show the 1STD1 sub-class of vehicle in three different paint schemes. STD22, above, has both upper and lower deck window surround painted white with a between decks black band. It has also lost its offside route number stencil holder. STD68 the subject of the lower picture, has the upper deck window surround and between decks band picked out in cream, whilst STD17 parked up behind carries the newest paint scheme, that of allover red with simply a between decks cream band. (J.H. Aston)

RLH3 is seen here turning into Scotts Hill, with the "Sportsman" public house in the background, at Croxley Green accompanied by a variety of other road users typical of the period. A visit to this location today would reveal identical surroundings but with the addition of a mini roundabout. Don't forget to pop into 'Allsorts' the well known model shop, which stands on the opposite side of the road to where the photographer stood. (R.H.G. Simpson)

Here's another oddity in the shape of a 60 seat L.G.O.C. built body, first worn by STL170 back in June 1933, now married up to a chassis built in the early months of 1942. STL2679 was a Country Area bus which in 1955 attained the distinction of being converted to a service vehicle and given number 1009J to henceforth be known as a trolleybus towing lorry! It is shown on a rainy day at the Pond Cross Roads in Watford during its short spell at the High Street garage. (Lens of Sutton)

RT4015 on route 59A waits at the lights beside tram 1909 and the cyclist aims for a quick getaway in this picture taken on the 3rd March, just one month away from tram route 42 being replaced by bus route 190. The setting is Thornton Heath Pond, a busy part of the Brighton Road, well known to vintage motor car drivers.
(D. Trevor Rowe)

Fourteen years have elapsed since its first entry into service but T674 still looks in pristine condition, although covered in dust, parked outside Windsor garage. It is nice to be reminded of how WR garage used to look with the name of the garage proudly standing astride two London Transport signs in this view taken on the 13th September. The 704 was the first Green Line route to receive the new RF coaches and so this picture was probably taken with a view to historic record. (Lyndon Rowe)

Parked at Waterloo, RTL772 operates out of Chalk Farm garage on route 196 having worked in from Tufnell Park. This is two days before the route was extended south to Norwood Junction but already an RTL has replaced the previously used SRTs. (J.H. Aston)

D170 is still carrying its previous paint scheme worn when in use as a Green Line vehicle. Now relegated to use as a bus on Central Area routes it is seen here at Clapham Common Old Town whilst working on route 5. This is a last day photograph since, as part of the tram replacement scheme on 7th January 1951, this Saturday and Sunday only route was replaced by 189A which also absorbed part of the 6 tram service.

At the beginning of the year under review only eight lowbridge examples of the once eleven hundred plus class of ST were licensed for PSV work. These were ST136, 140, 141, 157, 162, 163, 1089 and 1090 and during the year the number was depleted even further by the withdrawal from service of ST136 and ST1090. One of the very last STs to be withdrawn in October 1952 was ST157 pictured here on lowbridge route 410, once the haunt of the "Godstone" STL type and by this time operated by the new RLH class. RT1741 stands alongside in this view taken at Bromley North on 14th August.

(J.H. Aston)

It is the 3rd June and the photographer visits Chislehurst where he finds LT1197 working from Bromley garage. Well dressed, well behaved schoolgirls calmly board the bus giving a period flavour to the shot. (J.H. Aston)

RT3070 is seen here performing on the Circular Tour of London route 'J', which commenced in May, together with the other Festival of Britain special services. The four RTs which in 1950 had toured parts of Europe promoting the Festival were selected to operate this special service. Thus these 'GB' plated buses had a very high profile in their early life. (Roy Marshall)

Route 203 started running from Hanworth to Hounslow Central in February 1951 and then in July was altered to operate from Twickenham to Hatton Cross. In its early days it was normally allocated STLs specially drafted into Hounslow for the purpose but here it is worked by RT856 before the July change. The gentleman on the pavement is obviously attracted by the "Utility Suitings" displayed in the tailor's window. (A.B. Cross)

Nearly completed Thornton Heath garage provides the backdrop to RT1859. This bus had spent its first eight months in storage at the parking area adjacent to Edgware garage unlike most of its contemporaries which had entered service at Wandsworth the previous October before being transferred to Thornton Heath in April. (Roy Marshall)

Craven bodied RT1410 is seen working from Watford High Street garage on its journey from New Barnet to Leavesden on route 306, when passing the Associated British Picture Corporation Limited premises in Borehamwood.
(J.G.S. Smith collection)

G329 leads a convoy of buses taking home the punters and at least one clown (on the right of the picture) from the Epsom Race Course to Morden. G156 is the third vehicle in this queue of a mixture of various types put to work in Surrey for the occasion. The Guy Arab was a type seldom seen in the London Transport area of the county. Nowadays, with the car reigning supreme, very few buses perform this annual ritual. (Lens of Sutton)

STL1704 operates from Barking garage on the irregular 23C route to Creekmouth Power Station in this traffic free scene. Interesting period cars are parked in the street and I love the coupe and the intrigue of the notice fixed to the lamp post adjacent to the bus which reads "Courtesy aids safety". (A.B. Cross)

Photographed here at Sevenoaks Bus Station is red liveried STL1127 working on route 454 from Dunton Green garage. Through the years it was a common sight to see red buses working in the Country area. It did result however in incompatibility of blinds as shown here where no route number is given and two destination displays are visible. (Lens of Sutton)

With blinds set for private duties, less explicit than the contemporary "Sorry Not In Service", one can only wonder why Bromley's STL505 is sitting here just in front of the bus stop for route 94 on which RT2123 is working from Catford garage. (Geoff Morant)

Golders Green Station forecourt on the 11th June is the setting for B22 waiting its turn on route 83 to Hayes Station. All the B class retained this older red and white livery throughout their London service. (J.H. Aston)

Taken at Golders Green Station terminus alongside the Golders Green Hippodrome now used by the B.B.C., a background which has hardly changed to this day. On 11th June Massey bodied G263 and Park Royal bodied RT1698 await their respective journeys to Chingford and Archway Station. (J.H. Aston)

STL2681 at Gerrards Cross is from the batch of 34 "unfrozen" vehicles. This bus is coded 17STL3/3 and carries the LPTB built body originally fitted to STL275 when that vehicle was new in December 1933. (A.B. Cross)

Seen at the Western Region station in Staines, SRT118 operates out of the now defunct Twickenham garage. This fine looking bus hides its underpowered engine and poor braking ability. STL2542 provides the chassis and running units of this SRT, the body of which would eventually be used to build RT4420. (J.H. Aston)

As with the south western corner of London, which was dominated by the D class, the eastern area housed much of the G class with BK, U, RD and AP garages all operating the class at this time. G410 with Weymann body is seen here at Romford, operating from Hornchurch garage.

A pleasant photograph of G210 standing in Bowes Road, Palmers Green in front of houses now demolished for road widening. The bus is operating from Enfield garage on the lengthy 102 route from Golders Green to Chingford. Enfield garage had a long association with route 102 although situated some miles from the route. The extended bonnet required on a Guy Arab II to house the six cylinder Gardner engine is clearly visible.

An unattended RT130 stands in the brilliant spring sunshine outside Putney Bridge Station awaiting its turn to the Surrey destination of Epsom Station.

Early December at Ilford Hill just west of Ilford Broadway and STL1770, a 4/9STL14 variant, works the Sunday afternoon route 25A from Seven Kings garage, a shed not normally associated with the STL type. (A.B. Cross)

The date is the 10th of February and Ideal Home Exhibition time is approaching. RLH6, delivered the previous year together with the rest of this batch of 20 vehicles, is photographed in Watford at the rear of Leavesden Road garage in Copswood Road. The photograph clearly shows the chrome plated radiator fitted to these Weymann lowbridge bodied vehicles. They were intended for the Midland General Company but taken over by the L.T.E. due to the urgent need for such vehicles. (D.W.K. Jones)

A superb rear end view of ST1089 which shows signs of various adaptations over the years. The bus started life with the Amersham and District Motor Bus and Haulage Company Ltd. in April 1930 in a maroon and cream livery. It is seen here in the standard Country area livery used during and just after World War II and with only a few months service left to complete prior to its withdrawal in September. A front offside photograph of this vehicle appeared on page 117 of the 1949 book of this series. Finally, nostalgia will doubtlessly be aroused by the Wallace Heaton advert which was one of a series of stunning puns which appeared in this position on buses of the period. (A.B. Cross)

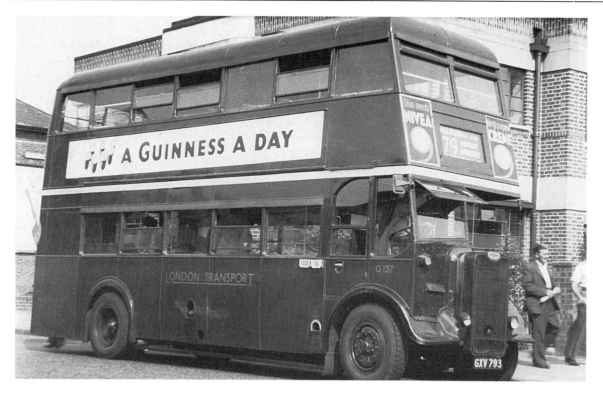

G137 is one of a pair, the other being G138, which were delivered in the first half of 1945 with Weymann all metal framed bodies, complete with winding type windows. Originally fitted with wooden slatted seats, these were replaced with moquette type in March 1948. The driver turns the blind ready for the return journey from Alperton to North Wembley. This Guy Arab spent its last years in Ceylon with South Western Omnibus Company, being re-registered IC1552. (A.B. Cross)

On lst June 1951 one of the local operators in Slough, J.A. Perry, was taken over partly by Thames Valley and partly by London Transport. To replace his peak hour services from Windsor to Slough Trading Estate, LT introduced routes 407 and 407A and allocated 1 STL and 1 T. Here T636 performs the duty on 18th October in High Street, Slough. The "Keep Left" sign is of rather more solid construction than present day plastic versions but was more likely to damage your vehicle. (A.B. Cross)

STL1420 works a Festival Extra service as shown by the typical blinds on route 19 between Clapham Junction and Battersea garage which was a short walk away from the Festival Gardens in Battersea Park. Interestingly, although this shuttle was at the southern end of the route, the bus is provided by the northern garage (Holloway). Holloway's standard allocation of RT is shown by the bus behind. (A.B. Cross)

LPTB standard bodywork of the design being built in 1935 is fitted to STL691 which first entered service in January of that year. Sixteen years and ten months later it is seen here on the 27th November working route 6A from Waterloo Station to Hackney Wick. This was chiefly an operation intended to supplement the 6 for City workers and provide a link to Waterloo which was actually served more directly by the Southern Region's Waterloo and City Railway. (A.B. Cross)

Park Royal bodied RT1883 on tram replacement route 109 followed by a Saunders bodied example, RT4251. Recently disused tram track with overhead power collection wiring is still in place in this view taken on a Sunday or Bank Holiday at Thornton Heath Pond.

Seen standing alongside the buildings of Northfleet garage is RT2267, blinded ready to take up service on the special route 488A which linked Rosherville with Kings Farm Estate. (Lens of Sutton)

STL2467 still operating from Streatham garage in the latter half of September on a Festival of Britain Extra service on the 59A route. In 1953 this bus was sold to W. North reappearing later in 1954 operating for Premier Travel Ltd. of Cambridge as their number 94. (A.B. Cross)

Muswell Hill's Weymann bodied TD23 and Mann Egerton bodied TD83 wait outside Golders Green Underground Station ready for the familiar trip over Hampstead Heath to Highgate and Finsbury Park on route 210. (J.H. Aston)

An example of an early AEC Regal chassis now powered by an AEC 7.7 litre engine from a scrapped STL, replacing the original petrol variant. T22 was built with an LGOC rear entrance body in the same fashion as the preserved T31. It was then rebuilt to front entrance in 1934 and renovated by Marshalls of Cambridge in 1949. This and the weight restriction on route 218 over Walton Bridge contributed to its longevity until 1953. (Roy Marshall)

Q10 still sports its green livery in this view at Esher of the bus on Central Area route 218 operating from Kingston garage. Many red and green liveried 4Q4s could be seen in the Kingston area between 1950 and 1952 until ousted by increased numbers of the TD class being moved into the area. Interestingly this Q with Q53, shown elsewhere in this book, were two of the unknown number exported to Libya in 1954. (Geoff Morant)

RFW9 looks splendid in this view of a high specification coach of the period. Of interest is the road lighting arrangement whereby the lights are strung across diagonally from pillars to light the width of the road from the middle. This could be Purley Way where such lighting survived for many years.
(Roy Marshall)

Standing in Lordship Lane, Wood Green outside an apparently disused coach station which has notable ornamentation, Q145 operates from West Green garage on its journey to Finsbury Park via Alexandra Palace.
(Roy Marshall)

RTL1117 stands on the inferior road surface of London Bridge Street on the 21st May while awaiting its return journey on route 44 introduced in 1950 in replacement of tram route 12. Originally Wandsworth garage was allocated RTs but these moved to Thornton Heath in January 1951 being replaced by RTLs as seen here. It is little wonder that London had smog in those days when you consider the chimney stacks in the background! (J.H. Aston)

Sea cadets and St. John's Ambulance Brigade personnel all appear eager to get aboard T731 in this view taken at Chislehurst on 3rd June. (J.H. Aston)

For several months during 1951 the eight Inter-Station Leyland Cubs were put back into service to assist on the British European Airways service from Kensington to London Airport. Very little work was carried out on the vehicles for their new role other than the removal of the Inter Station insignia and its replacement by a rather insignificant BEA emblem. C113 is pictured here with another of the class inside Gillingham Street, Victoria garage.

Standing with the arches of Kings Cross Station as a background, RT4157, complete with crew, takes a well earned rest from the tremors of running over the then still surviving cobblestones on its route from Honor Oak. (Royal Marshall)

STL489 is seen here at the Post Office, St. Albans Road, North Watford, finishing its days with LTE as a 2/16STL18. The bus has only recently been overhauled and therefore has more than two years passenger revenue service still to complete before being withdrawn. (A.B. Cross)

Tram 58 was identically replaced by bus 185 from Blackwall Tunnel to Victoria via Dulwich on 7th October 1951. For the first three months, although worked by Walworth's crews and ostensibly WL vehicles, the route worked from Camberwell garage across the road. Careful examination shows RTL799 has a Q code painted below where the missing WL garage plate should be, presumably to indicate its temporary stable. This was some years before garage plates were replaced by this method of painted codes. The scene is Blackwall Lane and the bus like many on this tram conversion was not brand new, as shown by the cream upper deck window surrounds, but had been transferred in from Palmers Green who received new RTs. (C. Carter)

An earlier repaint into red with cream band reliefs was carried out in 1948 to seven 4Q4s including Q53 for operation from West Green garage on the 233 route, Wood Green to Finsbury Park. Found to be unsuitable for this route, these Qs were moved to Dalston garage for routes 208/208A, Clapton to Bow and Stratford. All returned to the Country Area in 1949 but by 1950 some of the batch were again in service in the Central Area, this time operating from Kingston garage as evidenced here with the Kingston railway coal yards as a backdrop.

Muswell Hill Broadway and LT1060 from Muswell Hill garage and RT2292 from Holloway garage share the familiar stand still used to this day in the centre of the roundabout. (Geoff Morant)

Photographed just prior to having an overhaul which would change its visual impact forever is D86. Route 152A to Chessington Zoo from Mitcham was a summer Sunday operation which only ran in 1951 and never reappeared in later years. (A.B. Cross)

A rather dated looking Weymann bodied lowbridge STL1053 keeps STL1834 and T718 company inside Guildford garage. The driver's restricted forward vision on the lowbridge vehicle was typical of many designs of pre-war bodywork and surely would present problems in today's driving conditions. (Lens of Sutton)

Route 8 was one of the Central London routes converted during 1951 to the wider RTW class – referred to as "ballrooms" by some conductors of the time. On 21st November RTW35 works through the City on its way to Old Ford close to its home garage of Clayhall. Nobody in the background takes any notice of the bus and the picture evokes memories of hurried lunch hours in town. (A.B. Cross)

Standing just inside a Country Area garage is tree-lopper 646J. The registration shows that it has been converted from ST40 but obviously the body is not a standard ST. In fact it is a Short Bros. body originally built for the Lewis Omnibus Company of Watford in 1930 and acquired by the L.P.T.B. in October 1933 with that undertaking. It was numbered ST1138 in the Board's fleet but in 1942 ST1138 received a standard ST body and the non-standard body was placed on the chassis of ST40 and rebuilt as a tree-lopper. It survived in this form until October 1952 and was finally sold to the Mitcham dealer, More and Porter, in November 1953. (A.B. Cross)

RT2026 of Brixton heads for Cannon Street Station against a backdrop of typical South London domestic architecture. A few months earlier this had been the duty of tram route 10 but now sleepers in the bedrooms are no longer disturbed by the clang of trams. (W.J. Haynes)

Fairly new RT3174 with an older member of the same class stand at the Kings Arms public house in Westerham on a warm day in summer.

A rather dismal day in April provides us with green liveried STL533 operating out of Watford High Street garage. Two months later it was transferred to Dartford never to return to the Watford area. The location is Uxbridge Station and the bus awaits departure to NORTH WATFORD (DOME) later referred to as NORTH WATFORD (LIBRARY), a terminus which became largely redundant when Garston garage was opened.

(Lyndon Rowe)

Once STL159, but now service vehicle 833J, a 7 ton auxiliary breakdown tender allocated to Hammersmith Trolleybus depot. Note the semaphore type indicators and the design of the cab which appears to be a cross between a later STL and a pre-war RT.

Pictured here at Windsor Castle on 13th October is STL1927 on route 445. This comparatively short route had been converted direct from one man operation with Cs to crew operation with STLs in August 1944. (Lyndon Rowe)

RT795 together with another of the class stand at the Liverpool Street terminus outside Broad Street Station on the famous route 11, which was one of the most intensively operated routes in the years around the period covered by this book. (C. Carter)

Elmers End garaged STL403 waits at Battersea Park for its next duty on the special Festival of Britain service F which operated from Clapham Common. (A.B. Cross)

STL827 seen using the turning facilities for route 82 vehicles at Amos Estate, Rotherhithe. This particular STL was to remain in service to the last days of its class and then continue in revenue earning service with J.W. Lloyd and Sons Ltd. of Oswestry for a number of years.

On the 5th June RTL896, in accompaniment with "Tunnel bus" STL1866, stand in the sunshine in the vicinity of Athol Street garage, Poplar. Of interest is the cobble laid road, which in wet weather almost turned into a skating rink. (J.H. Aston)

C81 running on trade plate 974GC was being used as a staff bus from Hounslow garage at this time.
(Lens of Sutton)

An all metal N.C.M.E. body is carried by G164 seen here about to pass one of the well known J. Lyons teashops which were common to this era. Barking garage was the home for this Guy Arab bus throughout the whole of its working life in London. Eventually it received a new Duple Midland (Nudd) double deck body and was re-registered JWS602 with its new owners, Edinburgh Corporation, in 1953. (A.B. Cross)

This rear view of C8 shows that one man driver-operators in 1951 were not averse to walking to the rear of their vehicle to change the blind at the end of each journey. The adverts are also of interest. Whatever happened to Regent Petrol and was it only good for AECs? The Wallace Heaton advertisement, well known in the period, appears in this case to be misplaced on a single deck vehicle – or was that all part of the humour? The helpful AA route sign is presumably intended for users of the Tilbury vehicle ferry rather than the passenger one which departed from a different pier. (A.B. Cross)

The date is 7th April and LT1188 with a few RTs to the left is seen here at Elmers End garage. The driver is wearing the standard issue heavy overcoat which I would think was a necessity with the vehicle having no cab door. Elmers End garage was only to play host to Route 227 for another month as early in May the route's operation was transferred lock, stock and barrel to one of its pre-war operators, Bromley garage, thereby terminating the use of single deck vehicles at Elmers End for many years. (Lyndon Rowe)

On the 5th April STL1680 is seen with a background of delightfully detailed residential dwellings near the Pelham Road/Lennox Road junction in Gravesend. As shown on the "lazy" blind, Route 495 plied between Kings Farm Estate and the Plough at Northfleet in 1951.

(Lyndon Rowe)

RFW3 appears to have a problem with its semaphore type indicator not wanting to return to its holder but preferring to stick in a half open position. The bomb site in the background was typical of the City landscape even though six years had elapsed since the end of hostilities. (R.H.G. Simpson)

Q96 photographed at Fawkham Station whilst operating on route 489 to Gravesend from Ash and working from Northfleet garage on the 8th October. This particular bus was one of twenty seven 4Q4 nominated for Green Line work in 1936 following delivery of a similar number of 5Q5 type to the Country Area. With this new use, two of the modifications carried out to these vehicles are visible, the brackets for the Green Line route information boards and the fitting of the radiator grille at the front of the vehicle. Compare this view with other pictures of 4Q4s in the book, some of which did not get a conversion to Green Line use and therefore do not carry these refinements.

(Lyndon Rowe)

G385 devoid of its registration number and all its London insignia save for the fleet number, presumably in readiness for its eventual shipment to Southern Rhodesia where it was operated by Trans-Rhodes Services of Salisbury and re-registered S32733.

Seen here at South Street, Romford, an NCME bodied G256 does business outside the Ministry of Labour and National Service, the forerunner of the present day Job Centres. It is working through to Brentwood (Robin Hood and Little John) – the latter gentleman being excluded by the blind compiler – on a section of 247 once the province of single deck vehicles. (A.B. Cross)

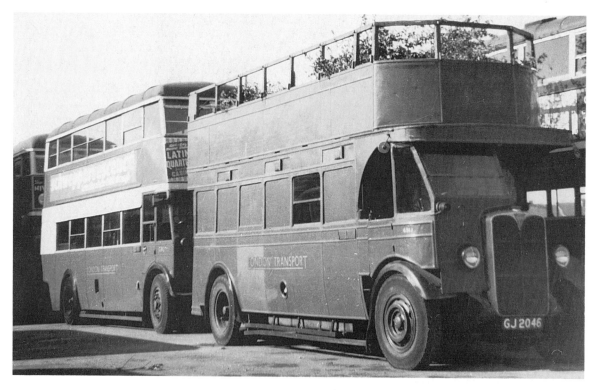

Once ST870 but now tree lopper 651J, hence all the greenery sprouting from the upper deck area, parked in company with unlicensed G82 and other buses at the time honoured parking area of Grays garage. (Lyndon Rowe)

Parked outside the New Victoria Cinema is RF2 showing its MCCW 35 seat body off to good advantage. Clearly shown are the glass cant windows at roof level, the ¼ drop windows and Green Line type Seating, which was fitted to all of these first 25 vehicles of this new class. (Roy Marshall)

At Dagenham, from left to right, are G245, G103 and G154 bodied by N.C.M.E., Park Royal and N.C.M.E. respectively. The two Northern Counties examples are of similar appearance except that the higher numbered one does not have ventilators fitted to the front upper deck windows. A variety of new homes were found for the trio after their service with LTE. G245 and G103 went to Western SMT, the latter being rebodied with a new Alexander low-height body. G154 found new work with the Ministry of Supply.

A contrast in post-war and pre-war private hire vehicles is provided here by LTC15, seen alongside newly delivered RF2 on land adjacent to Camberwell garage. The typical architecture of Bloxhams Buildings stands high in the background. (D.W.K. Jones)

Q186 is one of the twenty-seven 4Q4 from the original batch of 102 built for bus work which was converted to Green Line coach standards way back in 1937. At the same time the vehicles were recoded to 1/4Q4/1. In 1938 they all reverted back to bus work retaining most of their outside and interior modifications but losing the heaters which had been fitted. Ironically in this 1951 picture the Q is operating on Green Line work again, albeit as a relief on route 718. (Geoff Morant)

The long established 27A route to Teddington Station was the standard daily operation at this time, 27 being a Sundays only route to Hounslow. Not so old RT1730 operates from Twickenham garage in this view taken at the Highgate Hill stand at Archway Station. (Roy Marshall)

One of the buses which toured the Continent the previous year was RT1692. Here it is in use on the Circular Tour of London "Service J", which was the original post-war ancestor of the many sightseeing tours now on offer. (Roy Marshall)

TD59, with Leyland PS1 chassis carrying a Mann Egerton wood framed front entrance bus body, is from the batch of 100 vehicles, numbered TD32-TD131, delivered in 1948 and 1949. The bodywork is identical to that fitted to T769-T798 save for the lack of the sliding door to the passenger saloon carried by the Country Area AEC vehicles. The impressive buildings of the District Railway Station stand behind the bus at Haven Green, Ealing. (Geoff Morant)

Battersea's STL1690 works Festival of Britain service A from South Kensington Station to the Festival Gardens at Battersea Park. This was a route which, because of the popularity of the Battersea Funfair, survived into later years as 45A. (D.A. Ruddom collection)

In 1951 the District and Central Line stations at Ealing Broadway still had separate booking halls and the entrance to the former with the large canopy redolent of early Underground fashion provides the backdrop to T296. A Weymann bus body, originally used to rebuild an R class vehicle, is now carried in favour of the original coach body built by the same manufacturer. The bus is about to perform a short working on route 211 to Greenford. (Geoff Morant)

It would appear that Edgware garage have attempted to construct a skid patch similar to that at Chiswick in order to test the skills of their drivers as they take RTWs out into service on route 142. From left to right RTWs 235, 230 and 233 stand in the yard. By the end of the year all had moved to other garages for use on more central routes. Notice the upward curve to the guttering on RTW233 which was a distinguishing feature of the Leyland bodywork on these vehicles.
(A.B. Cross)

"Tunnel Bus" STL1852 in typical East End surroundings, complete with octagonal pillar box, resting in the sunshine before another trip through the stygian gloom of the Blackwall Tunnel.

Croydon was one of the garages to house the single deck LT class until their final demise from passenger service in London. Here LT1024 waits in the sunshine on route 234A. (Roy Marshall)

The 23B was a remnant of the several variations of trunk route 23 which survived for many years as a peak hour shuttle between Chittys Lane at Becontree and Barking where STL1704 is seen outside a cinema showing the latest war film "Rommel – Desert Fox". In the following year this STL was withdrawn and sold to W. & C. French the contractor of Buckhurst Hill for use in transporting their work force. (A.B. Cross)

On private hire duties from Chalk Farm garage, LTC19 is seen here at the same spot beside the long lived scaffolding as LTC18 was pictured in the 1950 book. (Roy Marshall)

STL1390 and STL1680 pictured here at The Plough, Northfleet on 25th April. The lower numbered of the STLs is a 3/9STL11 and was withdrawn from service in June to end its days with Cohens the scrap dealers. The other STL, a 4/9STL14 lasted till 1954 when it was scrapped by Norths of Leeds. The 495 bus is obviously using a rogue blind resulting in a double route number. (Lyndon Rowe)

During 1951 and 1952 a number of 10T10 type buses, until then always associated with the Country Area, were repainted into red livery for Central Area duties. At the same time they were modified by the removal of the saloon heaters and ash trays. The rubber covered flooring was replaced with new wooden slatted flooring. The passenger entry door was fixed in the open position and a route number stencil holder was fitted above the entrance. A few of these revamped buses returned to the Country Area immediately upon this work being carried out as shown by T577 on a short working of route 425 at Westcott. In November the bus was transferred to Loughton garage to perform the duties for which it had been prepared. (Lens of Sutton)

On the 16th October RT2600 stops en route to Greenwich at Surrey Docks with an over elaborate lamp standard silhouetted in the background. Route 70, which was introduced during July to replace the tram route of the same number, seems to retain something of the tram era in its destination which includes "VIA HOP EXCHANGE". (D. Trevor Rowe)

Although the double deck members of the LT class were but a memory in 1951 many of the single deck variety soldiered on until the following year. LT1168 is seen here at Barnes Common helping out on double deck route 33 from Hounslow garage.

"Godstone" STL1055 loads up with passengers, including one of His Majesty's military personnel, at Staines. The picture shows well the pre-war lines of these classic Weymann bodied vehicles.

Clearly showing the application of the London Transport fleet name is Guy Arab I, 3879 in the E.N.O.C. numbering system. Returned to its original owner in February 1952, the bus was later renumbered 1179 in 1954.

(C. Carter)

The date is 6th October and a rather depressing area of New Cross provides the background to Q152, a 5Q5 variety with Park Royal bodywork incorporating a front entrance in front of the first set of wheels, a somewhat hazardous configuration without doors. (Lyndon Rowe)

STL1898 is another STL which has just received green livery. It is seen here at Grays War Memorial operating the 32A route to Nutberry Corner. Up until 15th September 1951 this had been a joint service operated by Eastern National and E. & E. Benjamin who operated as "Our Bus" with endearing little Guy Otter saloons. Eastern National took over "Our Bus" just a fortnight before their service was taken over by London Transport. (J.G.S. Smith collection)

The only lowbridge STL19 sub-class body to receive an all over green livery with just a cream band in between decks as relief. STL2311 gained this colour scheme on its overhaul in September 1950 and, in the author's view, this arrangement seemed to suit the body styling. The bus spent the rest of its working life with LTE at Godstone garage and is seen here on route 410, which originally had played host to the "Godstone" STL7 variety of lowbridge STL. (J.H. Aston)

Photographed at Parliament Square STL262 is working as a Festival of Britain Extra on route 11 from Dalston garage. Several inner London routes were augmented by such workings readily identified by the "EXTRA" slipboard and "lazy" blind display. (Roy Marshall)

Q134, a Central Area 5Q5 with all metal Park Royal bodywork, is seen here with the impressive if somewhat altered lines of Alexandra Palace towering above in the background. (Geoff Morant)

One of the six STLs acquired by Hants and Sussex Motor Services Ltd. of Emsworth in 1953 and operated in Hampshire, STL2017 is seen in its more natural surroundings at Uxbridge on new route 204 to Hayes Station. This service had commenced on 25th July and was the first time buses had served the Judge Heath Lane and Botwell Lane route to Hayes. (Geoff Morant)

An unidentifiable STL keeps G118 and G7 company in this photograph taken in the parking area of Barking garage. G7 has now finished with earning its keep in passenger service and is demoted to learner duties. Both these Guys carry Park Royal built bodywork. (Lens of Sutton)

This photograph was taken at Beaconsfield which is the only place where routes 305, 373 and 398 all met up with one another. C56 would eventually be replaced by one of the new GS class buses in late 1953 but here it still has another two years running through the Chilterns in beautiful traffic free conditions. (A.B. Cross)

A further picture of one of the 3/1D4 sub class Daimler CWA6s with Park Royal much relaxed utility bodywork. D273 is one of Sutton garage's complement for route 93 and is seen laying over at Putney Bridge Station.

Route 287, introduced on 7th January, was the forerunner to the present night route N87 and successor to the night tram route 1. Here, in the darkness on a chilly night, RT2034 with RT3993 wait for duty clearly showing the route number blind beneath the canopy which was introduced with the RT3/1 class of body lacking the roof route number box.

SRT144 of Twickenham garage stands at the Kew Gardens Station terminus of route 90B. This group of routes received the final allocation of these hybrid vehicles before production ceased.

When full blinds were re-introduced to London in 1950 they appeared on newly delivered vehicles. However, by 1951 several earlier examples had been converted from restricted blinds including RT2487 from Cricklewood garage. This is Swiss Cottage long before the present one way road system was introduced but already 'No Waiting' signs have appeared on the lamp posts.

21st April and Perry Street, Gravesend, with typical newsagent's shop front of the period, provides the backdrop to Country Area STL1919. The stepped blind box display giving the complete route end to end was a fairly common feature in the Country area at the time.
(Lyndon Rowe)

T498 is another converted 10T10 bus repainted in red livery seen here working from Guildford garage on Country Area route 425 at the Onslow Street Bus Station in its home town and about to depart on the scenic run to Dorking. It was still to enjoy some scenery in Epping Forest in its future Central Area role when it was moved to Loughton garage. (J.F. Higham)

Pictured here at Uxbridge in company with a couple of RT type buses, Q104 still carries the modifications carried out for its short lived use as a Green Line coach way back in 1937/8. All the 4Q4 type so modified at this period kept these under used alterations until withdrawn from service. (A.B. Cross)

Photographed here at the Waterloo lay-by in June are RTW283 and SRT155 with a variety of STLs in the background. SRT class vehicles had less than a month to operate Route 196 as, in the changes associated with the conversion of Waterloo tram 68, the route was to be extended south to Norwood Junction in place of bus 68A and upgraded to RTL/RT operation. Here the SRT displays the blind intended for short workings between Kings Cross and Tufnell Park but conveniently accurate for the journey the bus was about to undertake. (D.W.K. Jones)

G436 is now operating from its second "home", Nunhead garage, although it still performs the same role on the 173 Nunhead circular route at Peckham Rye as previously. (D.W.K. Jones)

Aldgate terminus with Green Line RTs, an RTW and several trolleybuses to complete a busy view of this time honoured photographer's paradise. RT3231 awaits departure on route 722 using revised black on yellow blinds which replaced the amber on green versions which had proved difficult to read. (Roy Marshall)

Perhaps this picture was posed by the makers of Omo – did the nuns use it I wonder to achieve their beautiful white wimples? STL536 heads out on the Great South West Road towards Hatton Cross long before the present day industrial sprawl and Heathrow Airport noise made it such a busy area. (D.A. Ruddom collection)

The northern section of Charing Cross Road provides the backdrop to STL1574, a 3/9STL11 variant, working a Festival Extra on route 1 at Cambridge Circus. STL vehicles were not at all common on this route despite its long existence. (A.B. Cross)

The ultimate in touring coach travel, 1951 style. RFW11 shows off its Eastern Coach Works 39 seater, extensively glazed, 30 feet by 8 feet wide body. Of interest is the lack of a bulkhead to separate driver from passengers and the hinged door for all occupants to use. (London Transport 19242)

In March 1951 it became possible, following certain road alterations, to work normal double deckers through the Blackwall Tunnel. This wintry scene at Crystal Palace exemplifies this as STL1809 with special tunnel body precedes normal roof box bodied STL1634 on route 108 to Bromley by Bow. Both show the variation of restricted blind display unique to Athol Street, Poplar garage at this time. (C. Carter)

One of only two Bedford OBs, carrying the product of one of the many body builders who have passed into history, in this case Beadle. Indeed so too has the chassis manufacturer since the commercial vehicle division of General Motors is now known as A.W.D. Limited, having been acquired by Mr David Brown noted for building caterpillar vehicles and other specialist transport. (J.G.S. Smith collection)

STL494 finished working for LTE in this form as a 2/16STL18. The body is an STL3 type modified to fit its present chassis which has caused its recoding. The chassis, originally a 7STL, has been upgraded to its present coding by the installation of a diesel engine. Seen here at Marylebone Station on route 23 together with a Northern Counties bodied Guy. (S.E. Letts)

A nice peaceful country setting provides the background here to RT2264, a standard Weymann bodied example. Note the non use of the offside route number plate, a feature of Country Area bus operation. During 1951 the section of this route beyond Northfleet to Dartford was withdrawn and 496 became essentially a local Gravesend service. (Lens of Sutton)

Photographed passing the famous Chiswick bus body building and overhaul works RT75 may be on training duties although no 'L' plates are visible.
(R.H.G. Simpson)

An offside view of yet another of the 1948 Country Area to Central Area repaints, this time Q65 is photographed some way along the road from where Q53 in another view is pictured and facing in the opposite direction. Kingston Southern Region Station building appears above hoardings on the site of which now stands a row of shops including one which may well have been visited by the readers of this book in the pursuit of their interest.

Now demoted to training duties, RT24 proceeds beneath trolleybus wires as potential bus drivers are trained in the technique of the pre-select gearbox. The bus carries TH plates for Thornton Heath garage which commenced bus operation on 8th April 1951. (R.H.G. Simpson)

The wartime STDs were withdrawn from passenger service in 1951 and so the joys of travelling in this spartan upper deck interior was denied to the citizens of London. Unlike some of the G class, the STDs were delivered with the leather seating seen here but it lacked the comfort of pre-war moquette. (A.B. Cross)

RT3985 carries the distinctive blind used on tram replacement routes 57 and 57A as it runs over the still in use tram tracks in Vauxhall Bridge Road. It was considered necessary to distinguish the 57 as going (VIA BRIXTON) to Streatham and Tooting from the 57A which went (VIA CLAPHAM) to Tooting and Streatham. This was obviously not effective since in the following year 57A was renumbered 181. (Roy Marshall)

RT563 is standing within the confines of St Albans Country Area garage on the 84 Sunday extension to Walthamstow (Crooked Billet). It carries a Weymann RT3 coded body, being the classification given to the first variety of post-war RT easily distinguishable by the deep canopy and large nearside driving mirror.

D156 is another ex Green Line coach which once plied on such routes as 721, 722 and 726 from the Country Area's Romford garage till ousted by new Green Line vehicles. It is pictured here leaving Morden Underground Station forecourt as it continues its journey to Raynes Park on route 157.

(Roy Marshall)

Photographed leaving Epping with very little other road traffic in sight, STD124 is operating route 20 to Leytonstone from its home base of Loughton garage. (C. Carter)

G91, with STL494 behind, stand at Marylebone Station. The LPTB bodied STL delivered in July 1934 was to outlive, by two years the Park Royal bodied Guy, which dated from September 1943. (S.E. Letts)

A cold and wintry 20th January is the date T30 was photographed at Hersham Green on route 264 introduced the previous year from Hersham to Sunbury and extended in June 1951 to Kingston. This bus however is prematurely working the extended route by continuing from Sunbury through to Kingston on a garage journey. (A.B. Cross)

Red liveried STL443 helps out from Country area Hertford garage on Route 395 which forty years later was still running between Hertford and Ware. When Hertford garage had finished using the bus it was stored for a year or more before returning to Central area service. (Geoff Morant)

The dark interior of Athol Street garage seen in the background and the derelict area to the right of the photograph symbolize the typical East End before redevelopment. STL804, having had an overhaul earlier in the year, looks splendid with the addition of the slipboard below the canopy proclaiming "To and from EXHIBITION OF ARCHITECTURE (Lansbury) Poplar". This was the brave new housing venture exhibited in conjunction with the Festival of Britain. (A.B. Cross)

D168 is still sporting its Green Line livery although now carrying London Transport fleetnames having been transferred into the Central Area late the previous year when new RT type buses were delivered to Romford, London Road garage. The type of bodywork carried was of the relaxed utility style, being fitted from new with side route number box, a glass window to the rear of the upper deck and moquette covered tubular framed seating.
(Roy Marshall)

Festival of Britain service E operated between Victoria Coach Station and the South Bank and STL1618, a 14STL11 variety, is standing at its terminus on Elizabeth Bridge with the coach station in the background, a building which has changed little in appearance to this day. (D.W.K. Jones)

Seen here among many other parked buses in the yard of Camberwell garage are RTL1, RT10 and RTL6. All three buses are being used as training vehicles for tram drivers and on completion of the final tram conversion in 1952 they would be put back to passenger service, in many cases on the routes whose drivers they had been used to train. (D.W.K. Jones)

T776 operating here from Two Waters garage on route 322, a route that still runs today from Watford to Hemel Hempstead. The Ruislip Lido bound RTW29 behind stands at a temporary dolly stop here in Woodford Road at Watford Junction. (Geoff Morant)

T745 shows off its typically Weymann provincial type flared skirt bodywork when passing through Esher on seldom photographed route 206. The chassis for this batch of 50 buses (T719-T768) was the AEC Regal Mark I incorporating crash gearbox and 7.7 litre engine. (Geoff Morant)

Route 32 at Raynes Park uses D159 another of the redundant Green Line Daimlers for its relatively short journey to St. Helier Avenue. In this picture the replacement of the "Green Line" fleet name by "London Transport" can be clearly seen.

Cricklewood was one of the few garages to operate the SRT class throughout their short working career. SRT60 depicted here was one of a small batch first delivered to Gillingham Street, Victoria garage for Route 10 and then transferred to Cricklewood some three months later. Although the SRTs at Cricklewood worked exclusively on Route 16, which blind it here displays, this photograph is taken at Golders Green Station and one can only assume the bus is on an engineer's rescue mission for another Cricklewood vehicle incapacitated at this spot.
(J.H. Aston)

Here we have one of a small number of buses which arrived in London in grey livery. D69 is seen here operating route 49 from Merton garage, in a livery more akin to its owners.

(Geoff Morant)

Q16 was one of the Country Area Qs repainted red during 1950 for service at Kingston garage. Seen here passing through Kingston it heads for Church Cobham. (C. Carter)

Weymann bodied G416 is pictured here in South Street, Romford with two interesting vehicles moving in the opposite direction. First there is the motorbike and sidecar, a common enough sight for this period, no doubt in the course of taking the family to do the weekend shopping. Then there is red RTL1044 on Country Area route 370 operating to Grays, which garage often borrowed Central Area vehicles to cope with Saturday requirements.

(A.B. Cross)

RTL277 is pictured here in Richmond Bus Station which has been a favourite place with photographers for many years.

Originally delivered in brown livery in 1945 and repainted into this red and white scheme during 1948, D117 is pictured here at Westminster. The body in this instance is by Brush. (Roy Marshall)

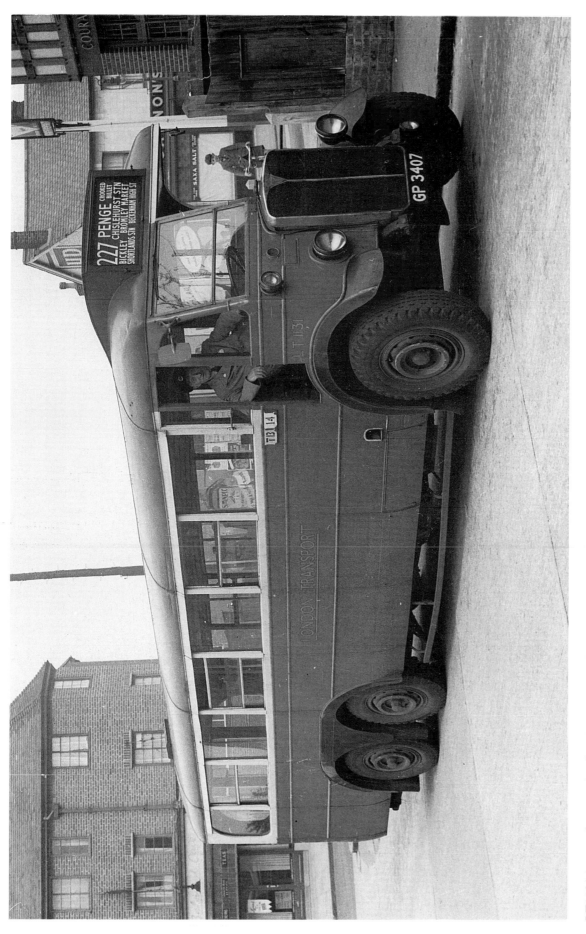

LT1131 is seen here at the Gordon Arms at Chislehurst now operating out of Bromley garage on a route long associated with this class. In the 1950 book this unique bus is seen working from Muswell Hill garage and in 1952 it was to move on to Kingston before being withdrawn from service. (J.H. Aston)

C24 stands out from its misty background in this dull morning shot. The 453 route ran up and down the hills between Chelsham and Caterham on the Hill and was operated by Chelsham garage.

Tram replacement route 190, better known as the 42 tram route to the unsuspecting passenger of the era. With disused tram track and overhead wiring still in place, RT1887 must have seemed a world away from the tram used up until early April. (Roy Marshall)

Originally delivered in all-over grey livery due to the shortage of red and brown paint, G120 was repainted red some few months after entering service. The chassis of this batch was the Guy Arab II with Gardner 6LW six-cylinder engine, as compared to Mark I chassis with five-cylinder engines used on earlier examples of this class.

The thirty-one Weymann bodied TDs were uniquely Muswell Hill vehicles for several years and TD14 arrives at the bottom of Muswell Hill on its way to Finsbury Park despite its destination blind. At the time "lazy" double ended blinds were being fitted to buses on this short but busy route and the driver has probably forgotten that his bus still carries the older version requiring nine turns of the handle every twenty minutes or so. The style of Barclays Bank shows a different age of banking to today. (Geoff Morant)

RT314, photographed here at Victoria, takes on a full load of passengers anxious to see the sights of London from a big red bus. Of note is the "J" plate carried on the corner pillar route holder, which shows just how well these buses were dressed for the occasion. (D.W.K. Jones)

A busy Sunday or Bank Holiday at the Wake Arms, Epping Forest. Leyton RTs 1485 and 2038 have arrived on route 38, the latter of which appears to be receiving first aid. Loughton's STD148 turns short on the Leytonstone to Epping route 20 while Enfield's TD49 departs down Woodridden Hill for Potters Bar L.T. Garage on route 242. The 10T10 in the background is probably also on route 242. (C. Carter)

The unique G30 which carries a Northern Coachbuilders body is seen in Wembley High Road. G30's original Park Royal body was destroyed by enemy action in July 1944 and the bus re-entered service in January 1945 carrying the only example of this manufacturers bodywork ever in LT service. The Fifty Shilling Tailor is of a bygone age and it is not surprising that the company was eventually forced to change their name to John Collier! (A.B. Cross)

Lightfoot's Mobile Snack Bar, alias Q2 seen in Leicester in 1951. When new this Q had a front entrance Metro-Cammell highbridge double deck body with the entrance in front of the front wheels. Sometime after being disposed of by L.P.T.B. in March 1946 the chassis was rebodied with a single deck coach body seating 31 persons and operated for Lindon of Windle, near St. Helens, Lancashire. In this picture much rebuilding had since taken place to adapt it for its present role although the pseudo AEC radiator grill is a quaint touch. (J.F. Higham)

Metro-Cammell bodied RTL610 arrives in Woolwich on route 122A from Erith which started running in February 1951. The Morris car behind seems well jacketed for the winter as is the bus which indicates it was a cold November. (A.B. Cross)

Just repainted green, STL1783 waits for business by the Queens Hotel in Grays. This particular STL was previously used in red livery on Festival of Britain services in Central London, evidenced by the giveaway unmasked blind aperture which has not been attended to in the repaint. (J.G.S. Smith collection)

This nearside picture of T404 clearly shows the handsome if somewhat ponderous lines of this classic type of P.S.V. Of note is the front wing and bonnet area, built as an integral unit, incorporating a larger than usual headlamp. This particular bus has lost its front bumper. It provides an interesting contrast with post-war delivered T733 parked alongside which appears to be smaller. The camera is not deceptive since the 9T9 was 7½" higher and ½" wider than the 14T12. Although now used by the Central Area the vehicle still carries the older Country Area colours of green and white. (J.H. Aston)

Q49 working on route 410 from Reigate garage is rather more unusual than the normal lowbridge double decker from Godstone. As unusual is the chalked on garage code and running number in place of stencils. The bus is seen here at Bromley North on the 21st May. (J.H. Aston)

Another Festival of Britain Extra, this time STL1562 on route 77. The bus is seen crossing the River Thames on Lambeth Bridge. A large number of STLs were overhauled and stored prior to their use on either the special lettered Festival routes or Extras such as this and all utilized this rather unhelpful style of blind design. (Roy Marshall)

Parked beneath some remarkable decorative stonework is LTC14c. By 1951 the practice of including the small b for bus or c coach on Country Area vehicles' fleet numbers had ceased but previously applied examples lingered on. When the batch were delivered in 1937, six were fitted with a "wireless" and the aerial for this innovative equipment to amuse the passengers can be seen around the roof at the rear of the vehicle.

T2 is seen here passing through Esher. The bus was first put into service in 1929 from Romford garage. By 1951 it was working from Kingston garage on one of the many single deck routes operated. This bus was the lowest numbered of the class to be renovated by Marshalls of Cambridge in 1949, continuing in service till 1953 in that condition. (Geoff Morant)

(above) Former Eastern National 3898, a Bristol L5G with ECW bodywork seating 35 working route 32B from Grays to Blackshotts Lane and pictured here at Grays War Memorial on 1st October. Note the new LT bus stop complete with E plates for the ex-Eastern National routes.

(D.W.K. Jones)

(left) Indicative of the mixed allocations on these routes Guy Arab I with Brush lowbridge bodywork carrying fleet number 3882 also works route 32B on 1st October.

(D.W.K. Jones)

Some of the little rear-engined CR class of Leyland Cubs were given a new lease of life in 1951 by the increased requirements of the Country Area. A few were allocated to Epping and here CR10 stands at the Green Man, Harlow ready to work a short journey on 393 across the embryonic New Town to Great Parndon. Behind is RT1017 working the even shorter shuttle sprig of the 396 trunk route to Harlow New Town, which was sufficient description at that time, although it has to be admitted that this picture was actually taken a few months into 1952. (A.B. Cross)

Passing the conglomerate of buildings making up the Houses of Parliament is RF9 in its as delivered livery of Lincoln green, grey upper section and red fleetname and lining out. Undoubtedly this was the most attractive livery to be carried by any of the RF variants. (R.H.G. Simpson)

With its days as a Green Line coach now over, T485 still carries its old colours. It is seen here at the Victoria Hotel, Muswell Hill stop on Central Area route 212 prior to being repainted red and moving to the south of London to give its passengers a rather better quality ride than that to which they had grown accustomed. (Geoff Morant)

A very angular type of bodywork was produced by Massey for the 49 Guy Arabs bodied for the LPTB in the nineteen forties. G358 is pictured here at Romford on route 247 to Harold Wood Station.

Before the Second World War route 32 was a major cross London route from Turnham Green to Raynes Park but it never recovered from the wartime economy cut which reduced it to a suburban shuttle. Here on 31st August, STL1731 works the basic core between St. Helier Avenue and Raynes Park and on Monday to Friday peak hours it would venture to Worcester Park Station.
(A.B. Cross)

Green Line liveried Q202 does a turn on Country Area bus route 365 and is photographed outside an interesting looking model aircraft suppliers shop at Park Street, Luton, adjoining the Brewery Tap. Would-be aircraft modellers should note that the shop is no longer there! (Roy Marshall)

Passing over Lambeth Bridge, all Leyland STD166 delivered in 1946 still has a few years service with the Executive before being exported to Yugoslavia with the rest of the 4STD3 batch. This class of 65 practically standard Leyland PD1 chassis with metal framed Leyland built bodies with minor LT requirements, such as the front destination and route number boxes, were purchased to ease the vehicle situation very slightly, prior to the post war RT deliveries which commenced in 1947. (Roy Marshall)

Four of Merton and Sutton's D class are parked here in Carshalton High Street loading up with an outing organised by the British Legion to the Harringay Circus on 17th January. To the left is D84 with two unidentifiable examples in the middle, one from Sutton, the other from Merton garage and on the right D216 announcing that you must see "All About Eve" from the beginning. A good comparison between route information blind apertures can be obtained from the two vehicles on the left, although the later type of Daimler never used the full set of apertures provided. (S. Sponheimer collection)

D145 on the 29th September, having recently had an overhaul which eradicated the Green Line livery it had carried since new. Previously operated by London Road, Romford garage on their Green Line routes in the East End of London, it now resides at Merton garage together with the rest of the first 181 Daimlers. Pictured here at Streatham on its way to Crystal Palace with RT4013 on route 133 heading for South Croydon.

(A.B. Cross)

RF15 working from Merton garage, clearly shows the folding air operated doors which was another new feature of this class that the intending passengers of the day would no doubt appreciate.

Upton Park received the wider RTWs from Alperton, Shepherds Bush and Southall in exchange for RTs during the year. This meant that as well as route 15, the Sunday 23A, Becontree Heath to Wormwood Scrubs, was converted and here RTW94 trundles through deserted surroundings on a wet September Sunday. (A.B. Cross)

STL859 of Sidcup turns at Orpington Station on route 229 which had started as a local Sidcup route in January with SRTs and then in October was extended to Orpington via the St. Pauls Cray Estate using STLs. The few commuters cars parked alongside present a different picture to the present day parking needs of a station like Orpington. (A.B. Cross)

Both these photographs were taken on 5th February at Gillingham Street garage, Victoria. The upper picture shows most of the 3STD2, Leyland TD7 buses with Park Royal austerity bodies at the end of their revenue earning service which had been entirely from this garage. They were delivered to the LPTB in December 1941 and during 1942. In the middle of this picture is STD104, to the left is the rear part of STD105 and parked a little further inside the garage is STD101 with more of the class parked to its offside. The lower photograph shows two vehicles, STD105 and STD103, leaving for storage at Potters Bar garage. All these vehicles would be out of action for several months until put to use initially as staff buses and later on as trainers before being finally withdrawn for disposal in 1953 to W.North of Leeds. (D.W.K. Jones)

LT1345 together with other single and double deck LTs gather dust from the Alpha Cement Works at West Thurrock in the scene above. A return visit a few months later on 4th June reveals that LT1345 has been slightly moved and adapted as seen below. There cannot have been too many ex London buses or coaches which have ended up with the hull of a boat sitting on top of them. It looks as though the intent might have been to drive the boat the short distance to the river – did it ever make the journey I wonder? (J. Pilgrim)

Another new class of vehicle introduced during the year was the RFW, utilising basically the same chassis as the RF class but carrying an ECW 30 feet long, by 8 feet wide 39 seat body. These were the first vehicles built to these newly permitted dimensions purchased by LTE. RFW6 with another of the same class parked outside the Royal Hotel in Woburn Place shows the semaphore type indicators fitted when new and the outward opening hinged passenger door peculiar to this class. (Roy Marshall)

(right) One of the most easterly points ever reached by London Transport was Shell Haven where former Eastern National route 35 served the oil refineries at the quaintly named terminal point of Shell Haven (Shell Cottages). In this rear view STL1521 waits in rainy Grays to make its trip down roads parallel with the Thames Estuary. (A.B. Cross)

(below) A nice line up of the new Private Hire RFs introduced this year is shown here loading a large party possibly in Cardington Street by the side of Euston Station. (R.H.G. Simpson)

RT409 makes its way over Lambeth Bridge on route 3 operating out of Norwood garage. This route ran virtually unchanged from Crystal Palace to Camden Town from 1913 for the next sixty-eight years. (Roy Marshall)

Here's a lovely nostalgic picture with so much going on around STL1465 at Dartford Market Street. Originally the bus was built with a Weymann front entrance body which it lost before the outbreak of World War II in favour of a L.P.T.B. built rear entrance body. The original body was then used together with STL1477's body to form a float for overhaul purposes. (Lens of Sutton)

In addition to the RTs which toured the Continent in the previous year, less illustrious vehicles made up the allocation on the Circular Tour of London. RT4068 is seen here whilst showing the delights of the capital to yet another four passengers. The incredibly traffic free conditions it encounters are of interest, as is the gas street lighting. (Roy Marshall)

Another picture which provokes the scene of the early 1950s with the ornate telephone box on the left. STL1054 displaced from Godstone by RLHs is caught here wending its way through leafless but sunny Addlestone on this early spring day. (J.H. Price)

Plenty of variety here at the Waterloo lay-by, now the site of the Red Arrow depot. In the centre are SRT90, RTW283 and STL462. To the right and standing back a little is STL1542 with more STLs and an RT family type vehicle to complete the picture. (D.W.K. Jones)

A peaceful street in Wimbledon provides the photographer with a chance to photograph the rear end of Qs 126 and 125 showing the pleasant rear end design of these vehicles and the emergency passenger door. The AEC "Q" chassis allowed a complete break from the standard vehicle being built at the time in respect of the arrangements for the driver and passengers to board and exit due to the positioning of the engine. (R.H.G. Simpson)

From left to right, STLs 1673, 735, 1657 and 1594 wait in the Waterloo parking area in Cornwall Road, which forty years later was to become the site of the Red Arrow operating base. All the buses are being employed on the special Festival of Britain services. (Lens of Sutton)

Pictured here at Windsor Castle is front entrance STL1033 operating the 445 route between Windsor and Datchet Common from Windsor garage which is sadly no longer with us. A Bedford OB service bus also waits on the stand at the end of St Albans Street. (Roy Marshall)

Massey bodied G359 spent some months as a learner bus after being withdrawn from passenger service. It had spent its entire passenger revenue earning life operating from Hornchurch garage before moving around three garages where new trainees were put through their gruelling paces. Finally this particular Guy was exported to Yugoslavia together with others of the type.

First delivered in the year under review is RF6, operating from Riverside garage. This was the first appearance of what in the ensuing two decades was to be the standard London Transport single decker. However, these first 25 vehicles were somewhat different in being only 27ft 6ins long and fitted with roof lights for use on private hire and excursion work. This vehicle is one of the examples fitted with semaphore indicators. (J.F. Higham)

Operating on tram replacement services and caught here by the camera at Farringdon Street terminus is RTL852 on bus route 45 which was better known to tram passengers as service 34. RTL920 seen in the background operates on route 168 which used to be tram service 26.

(D. Trevor Rowe)

A pair of STLs are seen here on service B, another of the Festival of Britain special routes. STL890 is seen in company with STL678, both bodies being of the STL5 variety, a standard L.P.T.B. product of the mid-thirties.

(J.H. Aston)

Having descended Muswell Hill from the Broadway, LT1012 arrives at the Victoria Hotel stop on route 212 to Finsbury Park. First delivered in April 1931 the bus has by now been fitted with an oil engine and would, by the time it was withdrawn in March 1952, complete nearly 22 years service all of which, apart from a rare loan, was at Muswell Hill garage. (Geoff Morant)

When compared with the picture of LT1012 above one can easily see the different appearance of LT1033 which is one of those rebuilt by Marshall of Cambridge. The panelling, beading and modern livery rejuvenated these vehicles considerably. Both pictures were taken on the same day on this very high frequency route.

The date is 12th May and somewhat bulbous looking Q117 waits on the 233 stand at Wells Terrace, Finsbury Park before making its circuitous way to Northumberland Park Station. The lamp post might well adorn the drive of some well appointed house these days. (J.H. Aston)

Parked within Amersham garage in accompaniment with a 10T10 coach is C40 which later in the year was to move to the southern area garage of Guildford. The blind indicates it has worked back from Chesham as a garage journey on the 353 Berkhamsted to Windsor double deck route. (A.B. Cross)

LT794 was withdrawn from service and disposed of to Daniels the dealer of Rainham in August 1949. Here on 4th June, almost two years later, in company with other unidentifiable members of the class, it still awaits its inevitable fate. (J. Pilgrim)

In the process of being scrapped by George Cohen of London and surrounded by trams awaiting their same fate is STL2052 on 3rd June. In its final form the STL was sub-coded 19STL16/2, being a 4/9STL chassis modified to take a composite structured, dowel mounted metal bulkhead STL16 type body in place of its original STL15 all metal structure. (A.B. Cross)

C50 awaits its next run up to Bengeo from the Hertford Bus Station, come car park. The lady passenger appears to be wondering why someone should want to take a photograph, but nevertheless positions herself nicely to complete the picture as she awaits the arrival of the driver to pay her fare. Journeys on this local Hertford route were often worked as a fill-in during layovers on other routes but it seems the bus was left trustingly open.
(Lens of Sutton)

The interesting background to this photograph, with the Gaumont Cinema and Scotch Wool & Hosiery Store in evidence, remind one of the High Street names of yesteryear. Park Royal bodied G200 completes the picture at Romford operating from Hornchurch garage on route 103, Pettits Lane to Rainham War Memorial. (J.G.S. Smith collection)

An interesting photograph showing STL473 operating from Hornchurch garage at Brentwood on the 86 route to Chadwell Heath with a City Coach Company lowbridge double decker in the background. (W.J. Haynes)

Mann Egerton bodywork of provincial type was carried on the last order of 30 T class vehicles to be built, classified 15T13, which were delivered in 1948. T787 working from Leavesden Road garage is photographed here at Uxbridge Station with what appears to be a full load and more passengers waiting for the next bus. This is Sunday 13th May and on Sundays an intensive service operated on this route in the afternoons to serve Harefield Hospital visitors. In the background STL2690 waits to commence a journey on route 351 to St Albans. (J.H. Aston)

Wembley Stadium coach park on the occasion of either the Rugby League or the Amateur Soccer Cup Final in the late Spring. As always in those days, something of interest turns up, in this case former DL36, registration GK8715, now rebodied as a single deck 31 seater coach and owned by H.C. Luff of Leatherhead with whom it survived until July 1953. (J.F. Bearman)

Q52 on route 497 which worked in Gravesend between the Clock Tower and Dover Road Schools. Unlike todays standardization on window arrangements, many different sizes and shapes are carried on these bodies built by the Birmingham Railway Carriage and Wagon Company. (W.J. Haynes)

The date is the 21st April and the Pelham Arms stop in Old Road West, Gravesend, provides an interesting background to T481. The bus, too, is interesting in that the Green Line fleetname has been painted out in readiness for a replacement London Transport one suggesting its days as a Green Line coach have come to an end.

(Lyndon Rowe)

Green Line Q234, seen here operating on Country Area bus route 365 at Luton on 23rd September, is one of 50 identical Park Royal bodied coaches classed as 6Q6 sub-type for Green Line duties.

A general view of the scrapping fields of Rainham with "Bluebird" type LTs and STs awaiting the torches of the professional dismantler who will render them as scrap metal in a very short space of time, although their wait has been lengthy. Daniels were at the time the main contractor to which time expired London buses made their final journey. (J. Pilgrim)

A Park Royal body is mounted on this Guy Arab II chassis to produce G88, seen here while allocated to Barking garage. In October of this year it was withdrawn from London service eventually finding a new home north of the Border. (A.B. Cross)

The crew of LT1181 seem very pleased with the fact that the photographer has chosen to record them for posterity. In the same manner as many photographs of previous generations the bus driver stands and obscures the garage plate. It would be most interesting to be able to name the crew in charge of this Hounslow LT Scooter; has anybody any ideas as to who they may be?

(Lens of Sutton)

Having been transferred in from Battersea garage, STL731 now works in and around Grays from Argent Street. Although the bus still carries its red livery in this photograph, it was, as with others drafted in to this new operating area, soon repainted green.

APPENDIX I

London Transport Central and Country Area Bus Garages

A	Sutton	HN*	Hitchin
AB	Twickenham	HW	Southall
AC	Willesden	J	Holloway
AD	Palmers Green	K	Kingston
AE	Hendon	L	Loughton
AF	Chelverton Road, Putney	LH*	Leatherhead
AH	Nunhead	LS*	Luton
AK	Streatham	M	Mortlake
AL	Merton	MA*	Amersham
AM	Plumstead	MH	Muswell Hill
AP	Seven Kings	N	Norwood
AR	Tottenham	NF*	Northfleet
AV	Hounslow	ON	Alperton
B	Battersea	P	Old Kent Road
BK	Barking	PB	Potters Bar
C	Athol Street, Poplar	Q	Camberwell
CA	Clapham	R	Riverside
CF	Chalk Farm	RD	Hornchurch
CL	Clay Hall	RE*	Romford, London Road
CM*	Chelsham	RG*	Reigate
CS	Chiswick (non-operational)	S	Shepherds Bush
CY*	Crawley	SA*	St Albans
D	Dalston	SJ*	Swanley Junction
DG*	Dunton Green	SP	Sidcup
DS*	Dorking	ST*	Staines
DT*	Dartford	T	Leyton
E	Enfield	TB	Bromley
ED	Elmers End	TC	Croydon
EG*	East Grinstead	TG*	Tring
EP*	Epping	TL	Catford
EW	Edgware	TW*	Tunbridge Wells
F	Putney Bridge	U	Upton Park
G	Forest Gate	UX	Uxbridge
GD*	Godstone	V	Turnham Green
GF*	Guildford	W	Cricklewood
GM	Gillingham Street, Victoria	WA*	Watford, High Street
GY*	Grays	WD	Wandsworth
H	Hackney	WG	West Green
HD	Harrow Weald	WR*	Windsor
HE*	High Wycombe	WT*	Watford, Leavesden Road
HF*	Hatfield	WY*	Addlestone
HG*	Hertford	X	Middle Row
HH*	Two Waters, Hemel Hempstead		

* indicates a Country Area garage

The above list is of all the operational garages available at the beginning of the year to which must be added the following, which were brought into use during 1951:

BN   Brixton   TH   Thornton Heath
GA* Argent Street, Grays   WL   Walworth
PM   Peckham

The garages mentioned above, except GA, were brought into use in connection with the tram to diesel bus replacement programme. GA was taken over from Eastern National, together with local routes and buses in September of the year.

Mention should also be made of the bus overhaul works at Aldenham although not an operational centre. Unlike Chiswick (CS), it was never given an official code. The decision to use this complex for this purpose was made in 1950 and although not completed until 1956, in the year under review increasing bus and coach activity was taking place at the site. Originally intended as an Underground depot and works for use with the aborted Northern Line extension from Edgware to Bushey Heath it had been used for aircraft production in the Second World War.

APPENDIX II

Update on Previous Volumes

This appendix lists information which has come to the attention of the author in respect of the books *London Transport Buses and Coaches* for 1949 and 1950.

1949

The picture of ST125 at the top of page 36 was taken in Chiswick High Road, opposite Turnham Green. Barnett and Barnett, whose white finished office building is seen to the left of the picture, moved to the Twickenham area some years ago.

The bottom picture on page 76 of ex-T594 was taken after the sale of the vehicle by Smiths of Reading to Chiltern Queens of Woodcote and is pictured on the latter's route from Reading to Wallingford.

1950

I should also have included John Banks in the Acknowledgements for this 1950 book – my sincere apologies.

The Q at the bottom of page 27 is actually Q151, confirmed by its registration CLE 174.

The upper picture on page 90 includes a 5Q5 rather than a 4Q4 as stated in the caption.

T244 on page 99 is standing in Kingsley Road, Hounslow rather than Kinsley Road.

An additional photograph which should be credited to J.H. Aston is STL441 on page 109. Also the vehicle behind STL441 in this picture is an RTW and not an RT.

STL2494 on page 120 is operating on route 335 and not 355 as captioned. In addition Leavesden Road should be spelt with three e's, a gremlin which has crept in elsewhere in the book.

The upper picture on page 129 is T648, not T684.